SHADOW & LIGHT
in the BORDERLAND

SHADOW & LIGHT
in the BORDERLAND

Selim Schaurer

Anax Publishing

Anax Publishing

979-8-9885621-1-5

Cover: Very special thanks to my friend of over fifty years, Bernard Plossu, for the use of his 1972 photo of a Big Sur forest.

Page xi: Special thanks to Shabana K. Dar for the incredible bevy of swans.

Page 28: Courtesy of Zastolskiy Victor/Shutterstock.com

Page 62: Many thanks to my friend Keith Kirk for the use of the awe-inspiring Via Lactea above the Pigeon Point lighthouse, Santa Cruz, Ca.

"Both light and shadow are the dance of love."
~Jalaluddin Rumi

"One does not become enlightened by imagining figures of light, but by making the darkness conscious."
~Carl Jung

"All this had been and he had never seen it; he was never present. Now he was present and belonged to it. Through his eyes he saw light and shadows; through his mind he was aware of moon and stars."
~Hermann Hesse

Contents

Preface

The number of named individuals that contributed to this volume are few, the number of nameless are many.

Foremost is Daniel Thomas Dyer. It is no exaggeration to say without him it would be merely a collection of attempts to express felt moments, vague inquiries, and the difficulty encountered when searching for meaning and what is real. It would reside in that which is destined for dust. He began with encouragement, finding some value in the poems I sent him. He collaborated in choosing the forty from nearly one hundred I sent him. I leaned on his vision and confidence that there will be readers, and most will smile along the way to, and including, the fortieth. He is an accomplished editor and book designer. He understands how punctuation brings clarity to flow, rectifying my disregard for it. My singular talent is recognizing a question and applying the mark. He has a refined aesthetic which makes what he publishes want to be held. Most of all he is a friend for a lifetime.

Kabir and Camille Helminski very tenderly offered their "finger pointing to the moon" with a couple of definite dos and don'ts. With an anecdote of an author friend who published *The Book of Secrets* with every page blank, Kabir emphasized that the title of a book of poetry is all important if you want someone to pick it off the shelf.

Shabana Dar Baker, my collaborator on a previous volume of poems enhanced with her beautifully attuned photographs, also is deserving as a named person for gratitude. Her belief in my adherence to including a creative expression that is palpable has never wavered and kept me writing.

Lastly and also importantly, I mention friend and verifiably trained and educated poet Tony Kendrew. He generously offered to read a larger file of candidates for the book and responded that after reading a few he took off his editor's cap and just enjoyed the read. Later his letters offered wisdom and the constructive criticism I was seeking. The short back page is a response to a statement in one of his letters.

As I step back to reflect on the past five years and the life span of this collection of poems, I wonder if there is something coherent, something I can say to place them in a context that might aid in their reading. Most were written after I celebrated my seventy-fifth birthday. In 2016 I "left home," having divested myself of most of my worldly possessions, to follow a calling that began in 1968 when I was introduced to the ideas of George Gurdjieff in Paris, France, and which continues to this day with the illuminated writings of Jalaluddin Rumi. It is a path to awaken to the most profound reality in this world of appearance, and experience the breadth of beauty and Love foundational to life. I want to say that every poem here is a love poem. Most are overtly so, and some may need a deeper reading to find it. They are grounded in my understanding of a spiritual reality and a Divine Source. They are observational, given that lens of perception. My heart understands Unity and sees it in the dance of light and shadow. My mind, at times, labors in duality. I apologize for those misperceptions in expression.

Selim Schaurer,
Ho'olawa, Maui, 2023

Abraham's Longing

Show me—bring it to the eye of my heart.
Let me see what Abraham saw,
The illumination that set his soul on fire
And caused him to weep
After all his failures and all the disappointments;
What never leaves his awareness:
A fire that is never contained
But never burns the eternal—
Consuming only what lacks Being—
That doesn't turn cold and ashen
As the embers die and warmth leaves:
The ever-living heart never bereft
Of Presence.

Absence of Moonlight

As the waves rise
And push their way to shore
Layer upon layer,

So too my awareness
this morning of You rises
Layer upon layer.

My heart lifts
From the ocean of decayed memories
With Your cascading Presence,

Washing me of last night's dreams,
Of the obscurity of sleep,
And the lull of ignorance.

A paucity of stars
And the absence of moonlight
Filled my night's sky with loneliness.

I could not find You.
No moonlight for my gaze.

Now I am warmed by Your sun.

Playa Coyote at Dawn

The endlessly arriving waves continue
Without caring what is before them.
Their only desire is for the shore.
Some meet jagged rock;
Others land on soft sand.
Like them I have passed though impediments,
Met the hard surface.
The soft sand has calmed my rumblings.
At dawn the receding tide reveals
A vast Pacific Bay
Curving to a far horizon
That draws my gaze over the edge.
I see now what wasn't seen in the dark.
Light clarifies, too, the inner horizon.
Palms lean, quiver with anticipation.
Cool breezes cover the expanse.
Dawn birds with their melodies
Are filling my heart with endlessness
And the gift of awareness.
May this day's experience
Be met with gratitude.
Some of what's dark is truly dark;
Some lit by stars and moon,
Reminding me that soon enough
Light will give way to delight
And the possibility of play.

Musings at the Tideline

At the tideline small mollusks
Rise from their entombment in the sand.
They wander the surface
Tracing awareness in furrows.
Their choices of direction
Perhaps reflect their longings,
Felt needs for their existence, or maybe confusion.
I see them as prayers, signs meant for heaven,
Petitions for fulfillment—a morsel of food, a mate,
Or, even better, a community of friends.
Certainly, like that note-laden bottle
Cast upon the sea to drift
Until someone picks it up
And reads the plea of a solitary existence
To be witnessed, and responds
Even beyond time and distance,
With excitement, curiosity, and love.

I'll Be the Wild Sea

Come with me to the craggy north coast—
I'll be the wild sea.
My winds will blow through you,
Clearing death from canopy and branch;
Preparation needed for new growth.

Come to my western shore—
I'll be the wild sea.
Your vista will be into the fall of light,
Into the heavens filled with the presence of angels.
They will sing to you like birdsong at dusk.

Come to my southern beaches—
I'll be the wild sea
That lifts you off your feet,
And you will know contentment
And the joy of dancing in warm waters.

Come to the heights of the eastern bluff—
I'll be the wild sea.
You will see in dawn's horizon
The first light revealing the gifts of the day.
And you shall love what has been brought to shore.

My love there aren't enough directions
To explain the tumult within this wild sea,
Nor the magnetic pull that gives rise
To wave upon wave upon wave.

Casting

I have never been adept
In the art of fishing;
I haven't the forbearance.

I can tie knots to the leaders,
Attach hooks, place weights and the bob,
Reasonably cover the hook with bait,
Even make the cast to the deep water.

But ask me to sit in stillness and silence
Simply to make my offering
Is where I come short.

It's been said that one needn't leave home
In search of fortune each day.
What is meant for us is already seeking us,
Eager to satisfy our need.

Jesus beguiled his disciples
With the notion that he
Would make them "fishers of men."
That took sacrifice, death, and resurrection.

Perhaps those are the template,
Accompanied by prayer to being found
By Being, for what swims in the depths.

The Heaven on Earth

Oh, let me hear birdsong!
Let them gather
In the dense foliage of green,
In the canopy of the tree outside my window.
Listen to their praise
For this life
And be refreshed.
Let me watch them fly
To roost as day departs,
To their nests in darkness.
I will say my evening prayer,
Prepare to join them,
Grateful for the day.
Up into the dreamtime
Fly without fetter,
Into the starlight realm
Of the night sky.
Feel the beauty
And the possibilities
Offered to my soul
By contentment and joy.

War in Heaven

There is a war in the heavens;
Battles taking place along fields of time,
On islands and continents of self,
Dawn to dawn, spanning ages.
Poets don't name it but refer to it with allusion.
It is very much within them and yet
It carries the nature of reality.
The life of this planet and solar system
Are at stake. Hellfires burn, hot and cold collide.
Ice encapsulates divisions of pain
Only to thaw when spring flowers
Push up and out of soil
seeking promises of Mercy.
Revolutions are continual.
We all die but for different reasons.

Capitulation

The hardest beauty to woo
Is the one that asks for everything
You think you own
And merely smiles
Waiting with open palms
For the endless baubles and tokens
You bring, and then tosses
Them into a dark treasury
Until you have nothing left
But the pain of separation.
And so, you place that
In the golden chalice,
On the silver tray, trembling.
It is only then you see
The sparkling eyes soften,
The ruby lips part
As the cup is lifted.

It is Thou
That feels the intoxicating wine
Coursing.

Penumbra

I am not
Even a shadow
Without Your light.

No soul filled with spirit
Without Your love.

Without your breath
No me to move.

There is only Your gaze.
Without that nothing is seen.
Nothing witnessed without Seer.

By Your word everything
Is formed from palpable nothingness,

The Nothingness of You.
Then You lend your Names

Without a name.
Haloed with light
I am helpless.

Dimming Light

(1)

There is no one here now but Thou
And what's left of myself,
Though outside the wind bends trees,
The water's surface is white with chop,
Clouds move like herded cattle.

Peace fills me as I face the spanning ocean
From the bluffs to the horizon.
I cannot hear the ocean-rumbling stones
On the rocky beach below.

That comes later in the dark of night.
These things have not changed,
Nor will they in the foreseeable future
Well beyond my witnessing.

(2)

His confusions and half-remembered purposes
Are on the plane to the mainland.
Five days with him, I am unduly tired.
What does he know of his former self?

Does he ground himself with tasks?
"What day is this?" he repeats and
nods as if he knew before he asked,
Wanting only confirmation.

One day at the table, amid ease
I asked, "How is your memory these days?"
It was like the question was never uttered.
He paused, silent for that long pause.

Then smiled and asked if I was ready
For a game of cribbage.
Like the cards he holds close to his chest,
Not revealing any discomfort.

Preferring to enter again this moment
With a new thread to follow until it unravels.
Or he solves some inconsistency.
His aplomb and courage are remarkable.

In his dimming light the world's beauty
Has not tarnished nor numbered the days
Ahead to be reduced in expectation.
Memories of his youth are clear and accurate,

Significant details welcomed with a chuckle.
His pride appears intact.
Ahead, behind—the line is unbroken,
Only now and the minutes and days before

Make no lasting impression.

(3)

She meets her confusion in different ways.
A sickle has mown gaps

In the perfect corn rows of her memory.
Sadness and depression are her tools.

Her identity has been her service.
Caretaking others has fueled her days and years,
Loneliness her nights.
Outwardly she copes with resignation spiced with humor,

Explaining that aging isn't easy.
She fills the waking hours with tasks,
Lengthens them with repeated organization.
Sleep doesn't come easy unless

The cup of forgetfulness
Is filled with wine; then it starts
Earlier and earlier, replacing breakfast,
And the synchrony with the sun is lost.

Stress is blamed, followed in time
by reduced capacities which doubles stress.
Fear has clutched her, helplessness,
Anxiety at the thought of no thought.

(4)

Two kindred souls on parallel paths
Through valleys of rose bushes
And the lapsed memory of their destinations.

Choice

When you wake
And the dawn outside
Is being greeted
With the raucous laughter
Of birdsong
While you notice
You're in bed with ache,
The kind that troubles the heart
And causes the mind
To loop like a mobius strip,
It might finally
Come down to choice,
Our singular freedom,
The only gift that can lift us
Above the web of dismal.
"This life is for the birds."
Do I give license to
This penal institution
Of disgust or listen intently
To the melodies of worship
through the window?

Shining

Let's say I have dabbled in quiet,
Walked openness until
The mind was no more than
Lonely clouds drifting across
An azure dome without horizon.

There was breath and heartbeat,
Only sensed differently.
All the while, my self knew
There was still distance
And yearned to cross
Into the heart of silence.

I think of it like an egg or perhaps
A fiery sun, a golden yolk.
Is silence ever born or
Is it ever primordial?
Tangential at instants
For the transmission of Being.

Am I merely another Phaeton
Who would seize the yoke
That marries steed to chariot
And steal my self to Helios's domain?

Can Emptiness ever be empty?
Isn't silence always present?
Light shines in the darkness
Of humility.

Consumed

Now it commands me even in sleep;
Rest no longer fully possible.
In every exhale it is there
and with each inhale it grows.
This pain has pushed its way
To the very marrow,
Invaded what I call "I."
And the agony of it is
No satisfactory expression
Comes to mind, no metaphor compares.
It's impossible to expel.
Nothing within sight, no sensation, no sound.
It defies my voice.
Neither quantity nor quality convey it adequately.
There aren't enough stars in all the galaxies
Nor grains of sand in all the oceans I can imagine.
Even the word "beautiful" is a beggar.
Only You embody It
And it is only with Your Face
That darker veils drop, and light begins.
I can only say, "I love you"
And will keep repeating it
Until there is no "I" left
And You have returned me to the womb.

Hypothesis

Just because the sun today
Has moved up into the clear blue dome
And the birds are raucous
And everything continues to crawl
Unseen through the fast-growing grass,
And beyond the blue and emerald sea undulates
With the languid rhythm of a practiced lover,

Behind this facade or within
This apparent idyll, this Polaroid minute,
The Great Wheel has not stopped at perfect.
The second hand and, for that matter, all hands
Are falling precipitously, and this center is lost.
As the perimeter is gained, the center is lost.

This glorious globe, this Singular Beauty,
This breathing life sustaining Being,
Is suffering an extinction,
And we have not paused
In our industry or aggrandizement,
Our appetite or our indifferences.

When does it matter that
What we dispel, disgorge and distribute
Is the acid, methane and poison
That rends holes in the fabric,
Is dismembering and disappearing life?

If ever there was a time to grieve
It is now, before we forget the truth

And dance to the fiddle while the flames
Turn the last greenery to carbon.

It is time to cry out
From the certain knowledge
We have lost our forests, oceans and shores.
Soon what we breathe will disfigure us

And turn us to slime like bleached coral.
Soon the ubiquitous electromagnetic towers
Will render mute and deaf every natural
Channel of communication.

Soon our careless ability to create
Substances and things that not only
Will not degrade and feed new growth
But are the source of dead zones.
Like black holes that
Suck with gravity the very light.

May our next breath be the one
Where we cry out with the experience of new birth,
As we did so in ours.
This time make it our heart

Awakening in this contraction,
This impending approach of entropy,
Our collective grief may not suffice.

We have been looking to
Ourselves far too long.
Those who persist in loving
Must step to the fore

And with the power of hearts
Embrace what longs for peace,
What seeks to return to the fold,
What has struggled for dominance.
So we turn to giving and, in so doing,
Surrender these billions of needs to control
And trust that all need can be met together

In the great Singularity of Love. (Cooperation.)

Loving What is Alive

Extinction is inevitable.
Let's be among the first to embrace it.

The world we are living
Is mired in excrement and indifference.
Let's be among the first to embrace it.

But let's not die with these bodies.
Soul extends into forever.
Let's start looking for it here;
We can awaken there.

If everything must change
To allow Love to flourish,
Let's be among the first
To sacrifice separation.

Our tree was planted before Time.
It still has good roots
And is preparing for spring.
Winter still has darkness left.

There is much chaff to shed.
Leaves still cling to high branches.
Let's let the sap of pride and power
Drain into cold soil.

As surely as the day is coming,
So is the light,
And light originates in Love.
Let's be just that and nothing more.

And wait to be stirred by the Living Force,
As we were meant for Loving.

Whenever Apocalypse Comes

Apocalypse: from the Greek,
 "To pull the lid off, Revelation."
For the moment
Let's try to do that.
Is it the end
That we are seeking to know?
What lies in the darkness waiting?
What can we know
By seeing at a distance?
Don't we have to
Go there with
All our faculties
Fully awake and with trust?
Let fear bubble around
In the final embers of light.
Let our heart tremble,
Yet step across the threshold
Remembering Love
As our bond to here, to now.
Leave everything we think we know
To learn what it is that awaits us,
That is our particular meaning
In this vast Unseen
Realm of Nonexistence.

The heart understands forever,
Can embrace the notion
Of eternal existence.
Love has certainty,
Knows no limits,
Has no end,

Only endings and beginnings
Fused together like our breathing.

Ogygia

If there is an atom of Odysseus
Inside of me,
Give me strength
To fix the rudder, set the sails,
Leave now with the oncoming tide,
Find open ocean and
Break the spell of this nymphet Calypso,
Whose power is to conceal;
Her wiles covering
The twin flames
Of Eros and Pride
That burn through the flesh
Ever hopeful of the love
Found in the heartland
We call home.

Pilgrimage

The old name for it
Still used on maps
Is Holy Island.
Separated from mainland Anglesey
By the Cymyran Strait,
At its end is the Holy Head.
Known for standing stones and burial chambers
For those who lived and prayed there.
It juts along the western shore
Into the Irish Sea,
A dynamic environment known for its currents.
Beneath, at the plate level is a major fault.
The separate masses moving
In opposite directions.
Past and future moving
Both ends into new oppositions.
I went there on a calm and sunny day
To bow my head into that holiness,
Then lift it and seek the far horizon.
My prayer: to find in that distance
The intended movement that would relieve
The blur of things held long and close;
Release the stress with the eye of the heart;
The old prayer, the old hope bowing,
Giving way to what could be felt
Just out of sight beyond the curve.
Following, perhaps, those old monks
Into the life that's beyond seeing
But beckoned with prayer.

Summer Rain

You have caused the clouds to gather
Dark and pregnant above the land,
Full beyond measure;
While beyond their shadow
There is light and the promise of mercy.
Just now the thunderclaps
Signaling the arrival,
While below everything shudders.
Thirsty gardens parched
Lift their need open to the sky;
Dry, crackling leaves expectant.
Flowers extend their tongues
Praying to be slaked,
Then respond with verve
And brighter color.
I, too, am dry as old bones
Having spent my energies
Releasing heat as fire,
Burned by recalcitrance.
Will I never remember,
Have patience and surrender
To all Your ways,
Accepting contradiction
And abrogation as self-induced?
You never waver,
Never leave me high and dry,
But invite me to turn again.
Upward, inward, open me
To mercy's resurrection.
Feel it's refreshment

Drop by drop upon my face,
Upon my tongue.
I love summer rain.

Summer Sun

It is broken, glass-sharp these days,
Hard and flamboyant like crystal.
In August the sun glares
Here along the Mediterranean coast.
It's a blaze, a penetrating flame,
An assault on activity and growth,
Sucking back its life-giving force
By perspiration and evaporation.
I am forced to the shadows.
Even there my eyes narrow
Assuming a glower without the glow.
Were we meant for this?
Life without veil, formless.
Is not life distinguished in proportions of light and shadow
Where edges can form?
Self is a manifestation of light contained by shades
Of meaning and of light.
What can we say of shadow-play?
Merely a flat projection through a screen,
Except that it indicates the real
And stimulates hearts.
This summer sun approximates death.

The Soul is a Bird

The soul is a bird caged in form,
Intended for flight:
To soar free of the gravity of things,
Those pained ancestral songs

Fledged by sorrow and tribulations.
It is the travesty of generations
That makes us earthbound
And has set snares.

Each soul holds promise and possibility.
Longing lifts it from the prison of the nest;
Dreams of freedom chart its course.
But it is Love alone that draws it nigh.

On a day when the wind blows right,
Let the call come from courage
To transcend pain and fear,
And the first tentative flight will be taken.

Once airborne no bird
Continues to fly in the same air.
Wings can bend to any current
Giving lift to all directions.

Freedom is gained, not given.
Conditioning breaks apart with that Breath.
Elation is initiation into the new life.
It is like a second birth.

Snares of blame and retribution
No longer bind:
They disappear into thin air
And the proximity of heaven.

Now the voice can reflect
Contentment in all weather.
Birdsong becomes praise,
Gratitude for a winged heart.

Cygnus

They glide atop their watery world
As if in continual prayer,
Heads bowed in supplication,

And within apparent stillness move.
Their motivations lie beneath the surface,
within and hidden,

Their plumage perfect feathered white.
When sighted upon the water
This whiteness commands attention;

It is the equivalent of light
And moves those who are its witness
To states that dreamers so often seek.

Known for love and love with faith,
One-to-one they mate and bond for life,
And tend their clutch equally with utmost care.

Love is at their core and in their heart.
They are shape-shifters, highfliers,
Far-transporters, realm-interlopers,

With their own constellation in the starry heaven;
Are consorts to kings and queens
And grace estates with dignity.

Rumor has it that they call to find their mate,
Whisper softly after mating,
And sing a final swan song before they die.

It is said the sighting of a swan
Means a nearby angel
Has a message for you.

I rather think them to be
Saints and prophets returned
To taste the fruits of past labor.

Dragons and Dragonflies

It is thought that dragons are malfeasant,
But in a garden, for the Chinese,
They become protectors
And bring wealth.

Dragonflies, on the other hand,
Are a testament to a garden,
Display its natural health
And the actions of love.

In spring they hover for hours
Locked in union,
Vibrating and vibrant,
Glinting in daylight.

Theirs is not some momentary exchange
But can last the lights of day,
Dipping occasionally to water
To deposit their treasured labors.

Buoyant and ecstatic in their need,
They are committed to
Its fulfillment; it is their calling.
Flying and floating in the face of gravity,

Inseparable they dance their passion.
The transformation hidden to the naked eye
Apparent to the Gardener.

Aboriginals tattooed them on their skin,
Representing freedom and enlightenment.

The meaning is said to be the awakening of intuition
And the transparency of the subtle realm.

Bee Stings And Behavior

Although you are no stranger to the Garden,
The Essence Gatherers will still ask,
"Do you belong?"
If you have not entered
in that lost state.

They will know your separateness
As fear and your fear as aggression.
At times, in recognition of your need,
They apply the sting of pain and poison
That it may become the remedy;

At others—sheer intoxication
With the scent of the Beloved—
They are driven to nearness, entanglement.
They give to blossoms the longing
To fall in love and bear fruit.

They impart the secrets of other to the flowers,
And have solved the complexities
Of generosity, mutual existence, and common purpose.
What marks them most
Is their attention to beauty.

They are grateful gifts to the Gardener.

Sublime

It's not an uncommon event for those who love
To walk where landscape becomes dominion—
Where the noise of human commerce fades,
As panorama and silence merge—
To linger there relaxed and find refreshment
In reveries and resolves;
At day's end feel emptied,
Their exertions rewarded.

Have you ever made this journey,
Except within and beyond the self?
Find the doorway in through silence
To the space no coordinates measure.
When the tongue softens and the mind quiets,
Thoughts break into single words,
Pass like windblown clouds revealing
Only sky and the concavity of mirror.

Is this the pathway to the inmost heart
Within the breast of human possibility,
Where breath and pulse combine
In timeless metronomy with Source,
As content and context flow free, unattached,
Emptied, consumed by and with contentment,
Transformed within witnessing
To love of Being?

Faith Requires Vision Not Sight

There are moments in every day,
Sometimes for days and more,
When I face the sensation of blindness.
These eyes are tired,

As is this efforting "I."
Little seems right.
Every direction looks dark.
My heart emptied of joy.

No bounce to my steps.
No clear path
Through boulders and brambles.
The Treasure is lost.

Familiar senses don't guide me,
Until a voice inside advises
In a clear voice,
"Death feeds on resentment.

Past thoughts are rigor mortis.
What is deserting you
Is the old lie crumbling.
Stay in front.

When the heart leads
You are healing.
Make room for the visitors:
Sorrow, anger, doubt, fear,

The lonely companions.
Breathe in, out.
The ancient emptinesses
Are to be felt.

With their passage
Is their service rendered.
Prostrate the ground
In your own original way.

You are a vessel,
Not a separate self.
You are a sky,
Not the passing weather.

As the old life falls away
New life is being born.
This is not error—celebrate, trust
This is a rite of passage,

Leading through darkness
As old life falls away.
New life is being born
With the turning of the wheel.

Others may not understand.
But trust anyway.
Praise the sky.
Embrace the ground; become still."

Emily's Garden

There are some exceedingly
Magical places in this world.
One such is Emily's Garden.
At first glance you might
Think it like any other
Small patch of tended soil.
A number of florae
Arranged in thoughtful pattern
By size, color, and texture.
But I can attest that
A love-child like Jesus
Was born there one day
From the passion that
Resides there buried
In the soil of longing.
After a morning's shower
Drenched with sorrow's tears,
Every flower leaned
In rapt attention,
Listening to every aching word
Released by Heart to heart.
Bees took that precious nectar
To their hives and made
Palliative honey from the revelations
Released from the blood
Of ancient wounds,
That carried forward the
Branching of familial misconduct.
By the power of the midday sun
Fresh sap started new green shoots growing.
Fruits long held captive began to ripen

To a sweetness seldom tasted.
While the Holy of Holies smiled.

Meeting

"You will be driven towards what you are going to meet."
~Imam Ali

This road that stretches out,
Yet is taken step by step,
Seems unfamiliar and odd at best.
So concerned are we with destination,
We rarely notice the tailwind
That acts as rudder too,
Course-correcting motivations,
Sometimes gentle, at times not.
Every encounter apparitional,
Understood as provisional,
Until we, fully fleshed, are
Ready to meet what has always
Waited for our arrival
At the appointed time and place
And welcomes us.

Together

I want to be with you
The way sun and rain
Are with spring gardens.

I wish to be with you like
The soft mantle of white clouds
That embrace mountain tops,

Like the bubbling joy of streams
Falling, tumbling over hard rocks,
Carrying soil to the sea.

I want to share with you
The dark, fecund mysteries
In fresh loam like earthworms,

To soar with you
As starlings do in flight,
With the wonders of murmuration.

I want with you
What honeybees and fresh blossoms are
In the exchange of nectar into honey,

That we might have the common instinct
That spawning salmon reach
In the graveled shallows of the birthing place,

Or with changing light the precise time to turn
And begin the inevitable migration
To the open sea and freedom.

If ever we find ourselves distant,
On opposite shores of a great ocean,
I will come to you with offerings of roses.

There is tumult in the daily grind,
Clutching hands and windblown nettles
Whose jealousies would steal this love.

But Light knows better.
It has cast warm rays upon
The fertile seed within us.

We have not lost the subtle knowledge
These intimacies within together offer,
Where boundaries are imagined things.

With grace lies the possibility
That the beautiful will always gain
Over what has turned to what is not.

Without You and Still with Me

I have these arms that do not hold you,
And these hands that cannot trace
The lovely contours and the
fine lines that mark your beauty.

My searching eyes don't see
The tender way you care
For what and who and how you love,
Or catch the impulse before you speak.

How I miss the fragrance
Of your skin and the way your locks
Fall 'cross your face, at times
Veiling the bright rays of your attention.

I miss everything about you
And yet you never left me.
Your soul in the image of your body
Comes in absolute clarity to the eye of my heart.

Sometimes still, in portraiture,
At others in a dance or
With words that drop me
To my knees in supplication.

And, if I'm especially lucky,
You come close as close can be,
And I am charmed by your mesmerizing lips,
And you whisper my longing

While I quiver with the staccato of our heartbeat.

My Need of You

When a single bird lifts its wings,
Whether to follow the course of the wind
Or traverse it,
What is unseen makes flight possible:
This is my need of you.

When salmon leave their deep home
In the ocean and migrate up rivers
To the shallow gravel beds at the source
Where they were born—within their heart is memory,

The very place of their birth,
Where they will settle their eggs and die:
This is my need of you.

And when the complicated caterpillar
Knows it is time to spin its chrysalis
Upside down on the underside of leaves,
Melting then into new singularity,
And with time enclosing with the ability of flight:
This is my need of you.

When the clouds, whether by torrent
Or gentle spring mist,
Drop their pure, life-giving waters
On parched lips:
This is my need of you.

Then as the multitude of drops gather
Into rivulets, into streams, into great rivers
Descending mountain and 'cross

Every vastness to the sea, clearing in the passing:
This is my need of you.

My need of you is like fire for wood,
Stars for the night sky,
The moon for the growth and diminishment of sunlight.
It is the need of the wind for treetops,
The ocean for waves and shore,
The sun to warm what lives
And give season to what grows and then dies.

There are multitude signs
Indicating the presence
And the sustenance of Love:
This is my need of you.

An Archeology of Love

If in some distant future time
The contents of our hearts
Were displayed in some clear and forthright way,
Our secret revealed in truth and living color,
What would those observers come to know?
What would they say to our love's story?
Would they see its Source?
Will that Hand be visible?

Will they say, "So this is how repose looks";
"They found beauty amid ruins";
"That intimacy was rightly guided";
"Surely a creation formed in Heaven"?

Will they trace the curving line of purpose,
Among the missteps and forgotten moments,
The pathway strayed then regained,
Pained pride and separation sundered?

Our entirety spread upon a tabletop
Or glass museum case showing
A finely crafted winged wonder,
The skeleton of we.

Each bone and sinew fitting
Like a map etched through remembrance,
Drawn beautifully with the precision
Of intelligence, intention, and inspiration.

Will they then say, "I see them in the night sky.
A cluster of light pointing East!"—

The brightly pulsing star that beckons—
And bare their own feet for the journey?

Fantasies

What happens to old fantasies?
I mean the ones you
Had your heart set upon,
Where your powerlessness and pain mingled,
Vacillating with ecstasy and anguish.
The ones too good to be true.
Where do they go?

Are they like old photographs
Hung in cheap frames on harsh sunlit walls,
Fading day by day, year by year,
Until one day you can no longer
Make out the smile, the arm
Draped lovingly around the shoulder.
Finally indistinguishable as to whether
It is a trophy photo of the old safari
Or the day you left home
For the university.

Maybe they reside in boxes
Of old magazines in the attic:
Advertisements of the dream vacation,
A summer cabin you'll build
On the property you will buy
One day by the lake,
Or the dashing outfit you'll wear to the wedding.
Boxes rife with mildew,
Pages stuck together,
Yellowed masses crumbling
By the extremities of weather.

Perhaps they drift skyward
In swirls from the flames
Of roaring pine fires.
The smoke of wood burned
To ash reaching distant clouds
Waiting to fall again as dust,
Cleansed by the rain.
Particles of soil for future dreams
To be planted by hopeful farmers.

With the consolation of forgiving,
I imagine them as sorrow's companion,
Commingling with joy's inspiration.
As a reminder that both are
Ever present, both to be welcomed.
As are always and never, advance and retreat,
Begin and end, strive and surrender.
Gifts from the source of dreams
For awakening a heart
To Presence.

Being

This life cannot be fully fashioned by a few flashing ecstasies.
It requires the stillness found in the darkness of graveyards
And the witnessing only silence can allow.
It has the need of the experience of sorrow and agony.
Their purpose is to bring to ground what would fly to heaven
And to set in motion the Great Pendulum.
Can you imagine the energy to create life
Out of pure Goodness, out of singularity?
And the pain of that separation never ending?
A wounding of biblical dimension would pale beside it.
Every synaptic transmission passing through
The womb of nonexistence,
Arcing the gap between two oceans and taking form.
When my heart contemplates this
Waves of pain and joy pour over my body's eye like rain,
While in the firmament they shine as stars.

Entering and Exiting

There is a courtesy to entering a room
And a gracious way of leaving;
Something akin to courtly behavior,
But more sacred while still earthy.
In every room there are angels
And souls in sacred conversation.
If, as you step across the threshold,
Your left hand is clenched around
Something and it is hidden,
And your right does not
Touch the heart in remembrance,
And you do not kiss the shimmering
Membrane of the doorway,
Then something dark comes in too.
What the eyes then see is plunder,
And what's in the left hand
Becomes a weapon.
The tender secrets being spoken
Disappear into silence,
And violence takes the space.
A subtle veil is drawn by the angels;
The chalice is no longer revealed.
Only ruins remain to be discovered
By some future heart in need.

If Not Inside

Where to find the courage
To meet with kindness
The anger raging now on every street
If not inside?

Where to find the calm
To face the fears
That run headlong toward destruction
If not inside?

Where to seek solace
For the empty pain,
The bleeding ulcers of loneliness,
If not inside?

Where to find the stillness
To the tumult and the raucous
On the descent to incoherence
If not inside?

Where to parse the lie
That would set each
Heart against itself
If not inside?

Where to find the breath
That breathes us
Into every waking moment
If not inside?

Where to find the sight
For the longing dream
In the graves of surrender
If not inside?

And in that potent emptiness
Bite to the core that fruit,
Release the seeds
Of consideration and contentment.

Exit Wound

Most often it happens
Early in life
When you are defenseless,
Or at the time
Of the first great change.

These are deeper
And lodge in the
Organ of understanding.
They startle you
Leaving you forever in fear,

Peering into shadows
In every stranger's eyes
Or the next room
Where mother and father
Keep their temper,

And you learn
To lock your door.
You are blind-sided
When the projectile
Rips into your flesh,

The dark round hole
Radiating pain
As the red ribbon
Of your humanity
Oozes to mix with the soiled.

If you are old enough,
You wonder if
You are dead or alive

Or will be abandoned,
And you pray for help
As you cry out in agony.
These are not the wounds

Suffered in ordinary war.
They are existential in nature.
But life and time move on.
With each iteration something
Does die in the flesh.

But these moments pass.
Scar tissue binds,
Is covered in shadows.
In some, whose longing is great,
A remarkable process begins:

Toxicity starts to transform
Into goodness,
Venom into remedy.
Light enters the heart
And it swells.

Arms embrace the body.
An exit wound opens
In the chest,
In the shape of a diamond
Faceted with the twin rays

Of Compassion: giving and forgiving.

Grandfather

Today we remember you.
Imagining how you must have felt
At your birth coming
Into a new body, a new life.
How you left the seeming stillness
Of your mother's womb
And with your first breath
Cried out, announcing your presence
To this noisy world.
How you who were created by love, cried out for love,
Vulnerable and in need of love.
We are all but short, sun-lit moments
Come from a long darkness.
What moves us comes
From what is hidden in our heart.
Our crying out is sometimes
Not so grand, but grand enough
To call forth answers.
Your voice was heard
And we are the response.
Your seed planted
In the long furrow of this earth
Has borne fruit and grain.
We are here because of you
And we are grateful.
We are the beneficiaries
Of your labors and lifelong caring.
Now you rest again in apparent stillness,
Finding a new body for your new life.
Yet still you will live on here

In our hearts and memory.
We whom you loved love you.

Lamentation

What is grief?

Is it in the towering flame of the funeral pyre
Alongside the river? The acrid stench and black smoke
Released by rotted flesh burned, turned to chalky powder
Of what once had form and held promise,
Beheld dreams and smiled concerned with the day?

In a brown, shriveled leaf clinging to a tree branch,
The very last of this year's foliage?
The empty house gone cold with only
A silent response from the missing presence?
The sullen stagnant blood of the bruised breast?

Or is it the action of a swollen river
That carries away the soil of a shoreline
Familiar to hearts, and tears loose
The roots of spring's seeds and summer's growth
To some distant oblivion?

Is it not, too, in the separation of what was
And what will be? The dark veil between
Becoming and timeless Being?
A threshold straddled beneath
A starless night sky, neither here nor there?

It's said the moon is a melancholy master
Whose only call is to what burns with longing
To find in daylight's warmth and providence
Color and verve of what's been lost in the dark,
To the far side of the world.

Do skies rain grief when war rains death?
How does earth bewail spilt blood?
That which crawls and walks, swims and flies,
Do they understand a sudden absence
And mark it with sorrow?

Or is grief embedded in expectation,
Hiding behind hope,
A bridesmaid's fear, or the consequence of denial?
One thing's for sure: the body cannot hide it,
Suppress it, and send it to the weakest without malice.

What is the metaphysics of lamenting,
And why do tears always come with it?
The salt in tears does redden and sting the eyes,
But more, the waters are for soothing and drowning.
Could it be the precursor to tender new life of fresh seed?
Or is grief finally the kindest path to a sweeter surrender?

by Keith G. Kirk

"You know what you want to say"

Yesterday I received a letter from a friend whose contribution to this book and my education is becoming invaluable. In it he said the above words almost in passing, but they stood out in bold above the remainder of the text.

Do I? The short answer is: maybe. The inspiration for what makes it to the laptop most often comes as a single sentence. There is always something mysterious about it. My hope is that it will be revealed in the attention and sincerity the words are given as content is added. Knowing then is a process of revelation.

The context that seems to produce these compelling lines has several categories of awareness. The most easily accessible is what strikes me as beautiful; be it intimate or panoramic. Another is the experience of worldly love. I have been fortunate to have the loveliest of muses who unlocked or opened chambers in my heart from which flowed a blessed brightness, recognition, and ancient memory. Of course, with love, as with much of life, comes pain, injury, and obstacle, with more opportunity to express what you want to say. Then there is the world "out there." By this I primarily mean the vagaries of politics, the ebb and flow of forces, light and dark, the contractions and expansions, we/they, power over and control, with little concern for others or for the living house we share. Finally, and perhaps most essential, is the sum total of Unity, of my need to understand nonduality, to find belonging where flow is realized as omni-directional, synoptic, and infinitely spacious. In my imagination, there is the world in which personal free will and Divine Will are symbiotic, and I want, at some point in time, to say it with a beautiful transmission of images evoked with words.

Milton Keynes UK
Ingram Content Group UK Ltd.
UKHW041840291223
435208UK00002B/15

9 798988 562115